D0611321

STRENGTH
FOR THE
JOURNEY

A Five-Week
Devotional

Tim Wesemann

The mission of CTA is

to glorify God by providing purposeful products
that lift up and encourage the body of Christ!

because we love him.

www.CTAinc.com

Strength for the Journey
by Tim Wesemann
www.timwesemann.com

Copyright © 2008 by CTA, Inc.
1625 Larkin Williams Rd.
Fenton, MO 63026

PRINTED IN THAILAND

Be strong and courageous.
Do not be terrified; do not
be discouraged, for the
LORD your God will be
with you wherever
you go.

Joshua 1:9

Strength for Christian Living

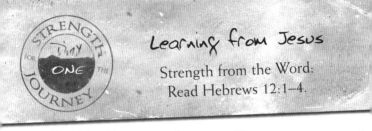

Learning from Jesus

Strength from the Word:
Read Hebrews 12:1–4.

Consider him . . . so that you will not grow weary and lose heart. **Hebrews 12:3**

Strength for the journey? Are you in need of some strength right about now? Life is a strength sapper. Pressures, decisions, and commitments sometimes overwhelm us. Throw temptations, sin, and guilt into the mix, and we find ourselves weakened and in dire need of help.

Thankfully, the Strength Creator and Strength Giver is holding on to you as you hold this book. He journeyed from heaven to earth and back home again. As a true human being, he knows how easily life in a world saturated in sin can weaken a person. And yet, our Lord Jesus lived a sinless life in our place and in his open tomb broke through even the wall of death, clearing a path to heaven for those journeying in his footsteps—that's us! What an honor to be chosen to journey through each day as a follower of Jesus!

But what about that need for strength you may be feeling today? Are you ready to take that need to the foot of Jesus' cross? Are you ready to ask your Savior for the strength you need for your faith journey? Then forgiveness, hope, and God's strength are yours through Jesus' journey into death and resurrection victory!

Strength for the journey is yours because you're his. Hold on as you read—and live out—these strength-filled words of help and hope:

> *Keep your eyes on Jesus, who both began and finished this race we're in. Study how he did it.*
>
> *Because he never lost sight of where he was headed—that exhilarating finish in and with God—he could put up with anything along the way: cross, shame, whatever.*
>
> *And now he's there, in the place of honor, right alongside God.*
>
> *When you find yourselves flagging in your faith, go over that story again, item by item, that long litany of hostility he plowed through.*
>
> *That will shoot adrenaline into your souls!*
>
> Hebrews 12:2–3 THE MESSAGE

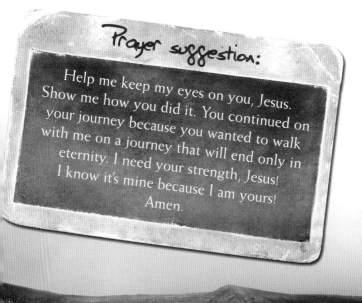

Prayer suggestion:

Help me keep my eyes on you, Jesus. Show me how you did it. You continued on your journey because you wanted to walk with me on a journey that will end only in eternity. I need your strength, Jesus! I know it's mine because I am yours! Amen.

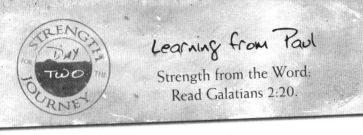

> *I live by faith in the Son of God.*
> *Galatians 2:20*

Rearview and side mirrors. Drivers use these safety features more than they realize. Looking at what's behind us *can* be helpful, but in some instances it can be anything *but* helpful. You can't drive safely by looking only in the rearview mirror!

That's also true in life. Each day brings with it the temptation to focus on past failures, hurts, and regrets. When that happens, Jesus responds quickly, reminding us to turn our eyes back on him and his plans for our future. At the same time, he's transforming our view of the past into one that reveals his faithfulness, grace, and forgiveness toward us.

The apostle Paul, once known as Saul, lived this truth. (You can read about how Jesus dramatically changed his life in Acts 9:1–31.)

Jesus transformed Paul's life from disgrace to grace. Once Paul had used his prestige and influence to do away with Christ's followers, but Jesus' love transformed Paul so he could do away with living for himself. Self-glorification and self-righteousness were out of the question. The strength for Paul's journey in living for Jesus Christ came from the One who transformed every aspect of his life. He could boldly— miraculously—profess, "I have been crucified with Christ and I no longer live, but Christ lives in me. The life I live in the body, I live by faith in the Son of God, who loved me and gave himself for me" (Galatians 2:20).

Instead of living in the past, Paul could boast Jesus Christ had come to live within him. The presence of Jesus changed both the present and Paul's hope for the future. That change was forever!

Yes, the call to follow Christ necessitates our commitment and transformation, and it makes that commitment and transformation possible. When Christ takes over, miraculous things happen as we live by faith in the Son of God, who loves us, having given himself for us. Through Jesus' death and resurrection in the past, we enjoy a future overflowing with hope, joy, and peace.

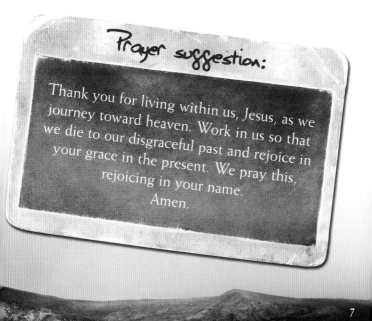

Prayer suggestion:

Thank you for living within us, Jesus, as we journey toward heaven. Work in us so that we die to our disgraceful past and rejoice in your grace in the present. We pray this, rejoicing in your name.
Amen.

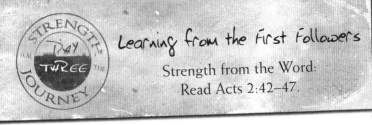
They devoted themselves to the apostles' teaching and to the fellowship, to the breaking of bread and to prayer.

Acts 2:42

When seeking strength for our daily journey through life with the Lord, we can learn a lot from those first believers, who placed their faith in Jesus after his death, resurrection, and ascension into heaven. This growing group of Christians knew the source of their strength, and they reveled in it while the Lord blessed them daily.

They prayed for and relied on God's strength. These men and women made a commitment to follow Jesus, even though it brought ridicule, danger, and even death to many of them.

Acts 2:42–47 clearly spells out the source of their strength to live the Christian life: Jesus! The first-century believers focused on his love, and they soaked up what they learned about him from his disciples and apostles. Relying on him, they modeled for us what it means to live as the body of Christ—encouraging and helping each other. They lived lives of worship. They . . .

• devoted themselves to the apostles' teaching;
• found blessing in the fellowship of other believers;

- continued faithfully in prayer;
- relished the faith-encouraging gifts God gave to them;
- supported and helped one another with Christlike acts of service and love;
- met regularly together in worship, praising God in every aspect of their lives; and
- lived out their Christian calling with sincerity and a joyful attitude of service.

Their God-directed lives opened many doors for the Holy Spirit to work in powerful ways in the lives of many other people—bringing those people to faith in Christ Jesus in greater numbers than we can imagine.

While living in difficult times, these followers received the strength they needed by focusing on the Strength-Provider. As he gifted them, they responded with lives of worship and service. What a powerful example they've left us as we journey through difficult days of our own, walking by faith in the same Lord who sustained them!

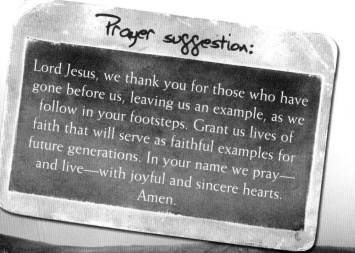

Prayer suggestion:

Lord Jesus, we thank you for those who have gone before us, leaving us an example, as we follow in your footsteps. Grant us lives of faith that will serve as faithful examples for future generations. In your name we pray— and live—with joyful and sincere hearts. Amen.

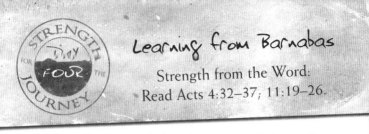
Learning from Barnabas

Strength from the Word:
Read Acts 4:32–37; 11:19–26.

> *[Barnabas] was glad and encouraged them all to remain true to the Lord with all their hearts.*
> *Acts 11:23*

Most of us have been given a nickname at one time or another. We may have received that name because of something we did or said.

The apostles gave a special name to a man named Joseph. He obviously had an amazing heart filled with gracious gifts, because they dubbed him Barnabas, which meant "Son of Encouragement." What a compliment! He must have been a huge blessing to the apostles. Sometimes we take the gift of encouragement for granted. Certainly we'd all love to surround ourselves with encouragers—and to be one ourselves.

Barnabas isn't mentioned often in the New Testament, but the life and salvation of Jesus Christ obviously influenced him. He had been strengthened in his journey through the encouragement of God's grace, as well as the encouragement of other believers. He couldn't help but respond in a similar way—by strengthening others in their journey of faith as he generously used the Holy Spirit's gift of encouragement.

Consider the blessing you receive when someone shares the gift of encouragement with you. It can change your focus, your outlook, and your attitude. Remembering that those who encourage you are responding to the encouragement they themselves have received from God can affect your faith.

God has gifted us individually in various ways. Like Barnabas, some have the gift of encouragement (Romans 12:6–8). Who is the Barnabas in your life? Has God placed you in someone's life to be a Barnabas-encourager? There is great strength in the gift of encouragement!

Be encouraged as you read this passage from Romans 15:4–6:

> *For everything that was written in the past was written to teach us, so that through endurance and the encouragement of the Scriptures we might have hope. May the God who gives endurance and encouragement give you a spirit of unity among yourselves as you follow Christ Jesus, so that with one heart and mouth you may glorify the God and Father of our Lord Jesus Christ.*

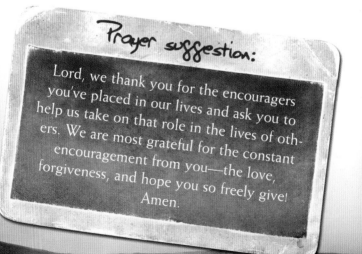

Prayer suggestion:

Lord, we thank you for the encouragers you've placed in our lives and ask you to help us take on that role in the lives of others. We are most grateful for the constant encouragement from you—the love, forgiveness, and hope you so freely give! Amen.

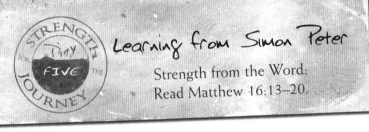
> ### *You are the Christ, the Son of the living God.*
> *Matthew 16:16*

The disciple Simon Peter journeyed with Jesus for three years while our Lord walked here on earth. Peter listened. He learned. He failed. He was forgiven. He imitated. He spoke. Like Peter's, our journeys with Jesus are founded on and often begin with a profession of faith.

Jesus asked his disciples who people thought he was—what he was all about. The disciples gave a variety of answers. But then Jesus asked another important question (Matthew 16:15, emphasis added): "Who do *you* say I am?" Jesus made the question personal.

Peter answered, "You are the Christ, the Son of the living God" (Matthew 16:16). Jesus knew Peter couldn't make this profession of faith on his own: God—the Faith Creator—had revealed this truth to Peter. Jesus came to earth as the Christ—the anointed Savior of the world, the very Son of God, the living God. Those statements envelope miraculous truths. Jesus is the world's Savior—and our personal Savior. He is the only way to heaven. He offers forgiveness for our sins, along with the promise to remember them no more. He gives us strength, and he himself is our strength. Jesus is . . . oh, we could go on forever. And miraculously, we *will* go on forever, because he is our *living* Savior—living *for* us and *in* us.

Who is this Jesus? Why am I following him? Jesus makes the question personal: "Who do *you* say I am?"

Are you ready to profess Jesus as the Christ, the Son of the living God? Maybe you've acknowledged that throughout your lifetime, or maybe this is the first time anyone has invited you to do it. Whether you have always done so or are doing so now for the first time, know that the Holy Spirit has created a saving faith within you. The One you profess with your mouth and hold in your heart stands as your strength throughout your life as a child of the living God.

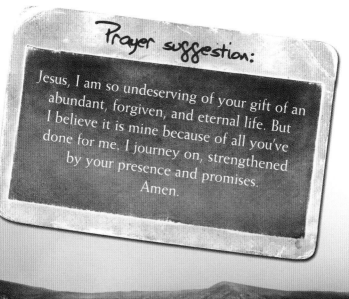

Prayer suggestion:

Jesus, I am so undeserving of your gift of an abundant, forgiven, and eternal life. But I believe it is mine because of all you've done for me. I journey on, strengthened by your presence and promises. Amen.

Strength from God's Word as I Live the Christian Life

Over the next two days, begin to commit the following Scripture to memory. Allow the Holy Spirit to transform these faith-strengthening words from head knowledge to heart knowledge. Sink your mind and faith into these words from the apostle Paul:

*I have been crucified with Christ
and I no longer live,
but Christ lives in me.
The life I live in the body,
I live by faith in the Son of God,
who loved me and gave himself for me.*
Galatians 2:20

*He said to me,
"My grace is sufficient for you,
for my power is made perfect in weakness."
. . . For when I am weak, then I am strong.*
2 Corinthians 12:9–10

I always thank God for you because of his grace given you in Christ Jesus. For in him you have been enriched in every way—in all your speaking and in all your knowledge—because our testimony about Christ was confirmed in you. Therefore you do not lack any spiritual gift as you eagerly wait for our Lord Jesus Christ to be revealed. He will keep you strong to the end, so that you will be blameless on the day of our Lord Jesus Christ. God, who has called you into fellowship with his Son Jesus Christ our Lord, is faithful.

1 Corinthians 1:4–9

Strength for Facing Challenges

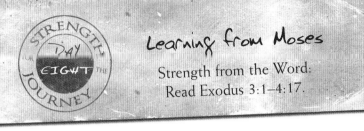
Learning from Moses

Strength from the Word:
Read Exodus 3:1–4:17.

I will help you speak and will teach you what to say.
Exodus 4:12

Look at these two understatements:

• Life is challenging. • The Christian life is challenging.

When facing your day, do you see yourself as physically, emotionally, mentally, and/or spiritually challenged? The answer is probably a resounding "Yes!" And maybe in more than one of these areas.

Because sin entered the world (Genesis 3), life became challenging, and it will continue to challenge us until we receive the gift of heaven and its perfection. As you hold this book, you may be holding on to some challenging situation. How good to know, then, that the Lord is also holding you and wants to give you hope no matter what you are facing.

What can we learn from the way God helped Moses with the challenges he faced? Moses went from the palace to the plains—once royalty, he became a runaway murderer. In today's Scripture reading, we find the Lord calling Moses, a senior citizen at this point, to lead his people out of Egypt. After decades of caring for his father-in-law's sheep, Moses was chosen by the Lord to shepherd Israel.

Moses felt physically, emotionally, and spiritually incapable. You'll find some of his responses to God's calling in Exodus 3 and 4:

- "Who am I, that I should go to Pharaoh and bring the Israelites out of Egypt?" (3:11).
- "I have never been eloquent, neither in the past nor since you have spoken to your servant. I am slow of speech and tongue" (4:10).
- "Please send someone else to do it" (4:13).

Moses felt ill-equipped to take on this challenge. But the Lord had a response for each of his excuses.

- "I will be with you" (3:12).
- "Who gave man his mouth? . . . Is it not I, the LORD?" (4:11).
- "I will help you speak and will teach you what to say" (4:12).

While Moses' lack of trust angered the Lord, God assured Moses he wouldn't face this monumental task alone. God himself would supply the strength Moses needed to face the challenges that would come his way. The Lord had answers for all of Moses' questions; in fact, the Lord himself *was* the answer! Any questions?

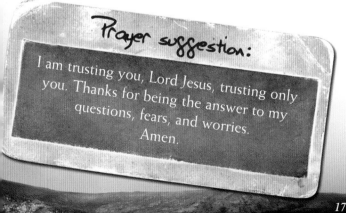

Prayer suggestion:

I am trusting you, Lord Jesus, trusting only you. Thanks for being the answer to my questions, fears, and worries.
Amen.

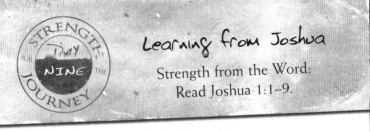
Learning from Joshua

Strength from the Word:
Read Joshua 1:1–9.

> *The LORD your God will be with you wherever you go.*
> *Joshua 1:9*

Imagine you're the vice-president of a corporation that employs over two million people. One day, you receive news that the president has died and left you in charge. On top of that, you don't own a cell phone or computer. You don't even have an office!

When Moses died, the Lord chose Joshua to take over where Moses left off—leading the people into the promised land of Canaan. Joshua didn't have a degree in leadership. And he certainly didn't have a Blackberry. (He probably had never even eaten a blackberry!) But he did have the Lord God Almighty—the most reliable help imaginable.

Check out the amazing promises the Lord gave to Joshua as he took over this leadership role:

- "I will give you every place where you set your foot" (v. 3).
- "No one will be able to stand up against you all the days of your life" (v. 5).
- "As I was with Moses, so I will be with you; I will never leave you nor forsake you" (v. 5).

How would you like to go into challenging situations with those very same promises in your hip pocket? You can! You *do* have the promise that victory is yours through

Jesus Christ. Satan will not be able to stand up against you, for Christ defeated him while nailed to a cross-shaped tree. And now Jesus promises to be with you forever—never leaving or forsaking you.

After giving Joshua all those promises, the Lord told him, "Be strong and courageous. Do not be terrified; do not be discouraged, for the LORD your God will be with you wherever you go" (Joshua 1:9). These words are a command with a promise attached. Joshua wouldn't be able to carry out the command without the promise. Neither can you.

But, good news! Both the command and the promise are yours, as they were Joshua's. Fill in the blanks, adapting God's words to fit your personal situation:

(Your name), be strong and courageous.
Do not be terrified as you (specify a challenging situation);
do not be discouraged if (specify a potential problem),
for the LORD your God will be with you wherever you go.

Journey with confidence, strengthened by the presence and promises of your Savior!

Prayer suggestion:

Pray about a specific challenging situation you will face today.

> *The battle is the LORD's.*
>
> *1 Samuel 17:47*

The story of David and Goliath is well known. What an account of courage, of hope, of victory! But sometimes we forget the details leading up to the point where David rocked (literally) Goliath's world.

Today's Scripture reading tells us that David worked two jobs—one as a shepherd and one as a musician for the king. His older brothers served in the military, fighting the Philistines. *Fighting* is too strong a word. They were actually just looking at the Philistines and their WWF champion, Goliath. The Israelite army stood looking across the valley at the enemy, shaking in their army-issued sandals. Every time Goliath belched, the army ran in fear!

So along came young David bringing bread and cheese to his brothers, just as his father asked him to do. His brothers were on the frontline in battle, and, well, it wasn't much of a frontline or a battle either. David arrived, saw his brothers shaking and quaking, and felt shocked that they would let Goliath "defy the armies of the living God" (1 Samuel 17:26).

David acted immediately. He approached King Saul and asked permission to take care of this pesky problem.

He reminded the king that as a shepherd he had regularly battled lions and tigers and bears, oh my! (Tigers? Not so much.) So Saul gave the rookie a shot—and one shot is all he needed.

David boldly turned to the giant saying, "All those gathered here will know that it is not by sword or spear that the LORD saves; for the battle is the LORD'S, and he will give all of you into our hands" (1 Samuel 17:47).

And the rest is history. Actually the rest is *his* story—the story of the living God, the God who acts on behalf of his people.

When you face giant problems and feel weak in the knees, get on your knees and take David's words as your prayer theme: *The battle belongs to the Lord.*

David had to put his faith into action. He couldn't just stand by passively. Instead of shaking, he began taking God's promises seriously and claiming victory in them.

Prayer suggestion:

The battle is yours, Lord. I surrender it to you and go forward in confidence as you lead, praying and trusting in your strong name. Amen.

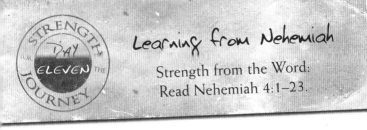

Our God will fight for us!

Nehemiah 4:20

Meet Nehemiah. While God's people lived in Babylon, exiled from their homeland, God called Nehemiah, the king's cupbearer, to an important leadership role—bringing his people home to rebuild Jerusalem.

Immediately, Nehemiah prayed for God's strength, blessing, and wisdom. He begged God for grace and forgiveness, because the people had run away from the Lord's will and ways. They had acted wickedly instead of obeying God's commands. Nehemiah knew they needed to return to the Word of God as they returned to Jerusalem in order to restore it to a place that brought honor to the Lord.

One of the challenges facing this man of God came in the form of detractors. (Haven't we all had those at one point or another?) Sanballat and Tobiah loved to voice their opposition to the project. They spoke to turn the people's courage into discouragement. While the workers stirred mortar, Sanballat and his crew stirred up trouble.

Rumblings of discouragement, and even surrender, entered Nehemiah's ears as his crew, the people of Judah, took the attacks to heart. Satan used their enemies to convince them the bad guys would attack and destroy them.

Nehemiah, filled with God's Spirit, ran to their rescue, supporting that crew, shoring up the faith and courage of those wall builders! He said, "Don't be afraid of them. Remember the Lord, who is great and awesome, and fight for your brothers, your sons and your daughters, your wives and your homes" (Nehemiah 4:14).

After placing God's confidence within the hearts and minds of the people, Nehemiah also placed weapons in the hands of half of them. They took turns protecting the wall and workers. Those who carried materials did so with one hand as they held a weapon in the other! Armed, yet working. Protecting, yet building.

Are tempting voices encouraging you to quit? Do you hear words of discouragement as you fight your battles? Do not be afraid! Remember the Lord who is great and awesome! Put on his armor, as you continue to go about what he has called you to do! Support and safety and salvation—they're yours in Jesus.

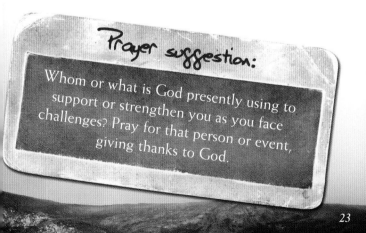

Prayer suggestion:

Whom or what is God presently using to support or strengthen you as you face challenges? Pray for that person or event, giving thanks to God.

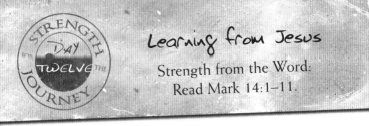

STRENGTH
DAY
TWELVE THE
JOURNEY

Learning from Jesus

Strength from the Word:
Read Mark 14:1–11.

Let us then approach the throne of grace with confidence, so that we may receive mercy and find grace to help us in our time of need.
Hebrews 4:16

In just a few short verses from Mark 14 we read about four major conflicts facing Jesus. In this passage we see

- Jesus facing torture, ridicule, and death by crucifixion;
- Jesus' enemies plotting ways to arrest and kill him;
- Jesus' own disciples complaining about trivial issues and their lack of faith-focus; and
- one of our Lord's closest friends, his chosen disciple Judas, selling Jesus out—simply to feed his greed.

As you read the verses, did you consider your own list of current challenges and conflicts? In reading about Jesus' life, don't you find it comforting that Jesus experienced adversaries and troubles very much like those we face? He lived in a sinful world—although he remained sinless—a world full of conflicts, pressures, and pain, much like our own.

Jesus knew about loneliness and rejection. He knows what it's like to feel swamped with responsibilities and to be misunderstood by friends. Jesus experienced physical pain, and he faced death—the "last enemy" of all human beings (1 Corinthians 15:26). The list could go and on.

Hebrews 4:14–16 reads:

> *Therefore, since we have a great high priest who has gone through the heavens, Jesus the Son of God, let us hold firmly to the faith we profess. For we do not have a high priest who is unable to sympathize with our weaknesses, but we have one who has been tempted in every way, just as we are—yet was without sin. Let us then approach the throne of grace with confidence, so that we may receive mercy and find grace to help us in our time of need.*

Jesus can honestly say, "I understand how you feel." And it's true! Combine that truth with his heart of compassion and his wisdom in knowing how best to meet your needs, and you'll receive comfort like you've never known before.

The next time you need some understanding (which is probably this very moment), stand under his understanding. It's a very comforting place to be!

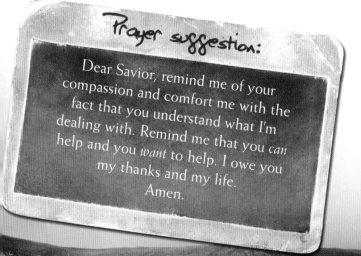

Prayer suggestion:

Dear Savior, remind me of your compassion and comfort me with the fact that you understand what I'm dealing with. Remind me that you can help and you *want* to help. I owe you my thanks and my life.
Amen.

Strength from God's Word as I Face Challenges

Over the next two days, begin to commit the following Scripture to memory. Allow the Holy Spirit to transform these faith-strengthening words from head knowledge to heart knowledge. Sink your mind and faith into these words from the Old Testament books of Isaiah and Psalms:

> *O LORD, be gracious to us;*
> *we long for you.*
> *Be our strength every morning,*
> *our salvation in time of distress.*
> **Isaiah 33:2**

> *God is our refuge and strength,*
> *an ever-present help in trouble.*
> **Psalm 46:1**

[Jesus said,] "Are you tired? Worn out? . . . Come to me. Get away with me and you'll recover your life. I'll show you how to take a real rest. Walk with me and work with me—watch how I do it. Learn the unforced rhythms of grace. I won't lay anything heavy or ill-fitting on you. Keep company with me and you'll learn to live freely and lightly."

Matthew 11:28–30 THE MESSAGE

Strength for Making Choices

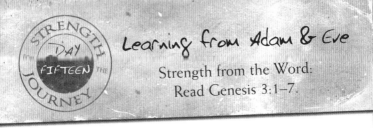
> *The wages of sin is death, but the gift of God is
> eternal life in Christ Jesus our Lord.*
>
> *Romans 6:23*

Wikipedia defines a *blunder* as a "spectacularly bad or embarrassing mistake—a bad decision with a disastrous result." It goes on to list some of the greatest blunders in history:

- The Edsel
- The Battle of Little Big Horn
- Hitler declaring war on the U.S.
- The sale of Babe Ruth from the Red Sox to the Yankees
- Watergate
- Adam and Eve

Okay, so the last one didn't make Wikipedia's list, but it's safe to say the others happened because of Adam and Eve's *bad decision with disastrous results.*

Adam and Eve had been given free choice as they lived in perfection—without sin. The Lord gave one command, however—not to eat from one particular tree in the garden. The consequences were well defined: death would come into the world and their lives. (See Genesis 2:16–17.)

You likely know how the story ended. Call their action a bad decision, a blunder, or a mistake, but the bottom line is that they sinned. With sin's entry into the world came worry, anger, addictions, relationship problems, hospitals, and death.

So what can we learn from their decision to ignore God's warning and throw God's command aside? We can discern that the Lord takes sin seriously and so should we. Also, sin brings with it consequences. Our sin leads to death:

> **The wages of sin is death, but the gift of God is eternal life in Christ Jesus our Lord.**
> **Romans 6:23**

Did you catch the last part of that promise? "The gift of God is eternal *life* in Christ Jesus" (emphasis added). Here, we sinners receive hope, good news! Yes, in Christ Jesus there is forgiveness for all of our sins! While the consequences of our sin most assuredly affect us and others temporarily, the gift of forgiveness and eternal life in Jesus affects our lives eternally! That truth gives us strength for making decisions, and it makes it possible for us to forgive those around us who have hurt us through their own sinful decisions.

Prayer suggestion:

Forgive me, Father, for I have sinned against you and others. Help me forgive others as I have been forgiven. I pray for strength in making decisions that glorify you. Amen.

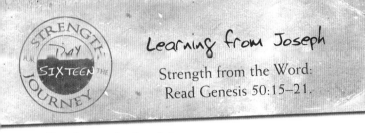

Learning from Joseph

Strength from the Word:
Read Genesis 50:15–21.

STRENGTH
Day
SIXTEEN
THE
JOURNEY

Forgive as the Lord forgave you.
Colossians 3:13

In the last three minutes, I've blinked, sneezed, walked, typed, swallowed, and breathed without telling my eyes, legs, fingers, lungs, throat, or nose to do any of those things. They are all part of my body's reflexes, mostly involuntary reflexes.

At the same time all our involuntary reflexes are at work, we are constantly making voluntary, conscious choices. In fact, you chose to read this devotion (at least up to this sentence)! Every minute is filled with choices to do this or that, to respond in one way or another. Thankfully, we don't have to choose to do things like blink or breathe. God takes care of that! If we had to concentrate on keeping all those processes happening while we were also living our lives, it would drive us to distraction!

All this makes me think. Wouldn't it be nice to have involuntary faith reflexes? In one area, I guess we do. *All* creation cries out its praise to God, from every blade of grass to every individual's physical body. "The heavens declare the glory of God" (Psalm 19:1).

But what about other possible involuntary faith reflexes? Involuntary reflexes for compassion, joy, and faithfulness would change our lives, and our world, in astonishing ways. And what about the choice to forgive? Why do we too often turn that into such a difficult choice when we have been fully forgiven by Jesus Christ? His forgiveness is mind-boggling! His death on the cross won forgiveness for *all* our sins—past, present, and future. Forgiveness is a great miracle. And it's also a choice we can have as we live with others.

One great Old Testament story of forgiveness is found in the life and faith of Joseph (Genesis 50:15–21). After his brothers abused Joseph, selling him off into slavery, he calmly responded, "You intended to harm me, but God intended it for good to accomplish what is now being done, the saving of many lives" (Genesis 50:20). Joseph's forgiveness flowed from a faith responding to the gracious forgiveness he knew he had received freely from the Lord.

Yes, forgiveness is for giving!

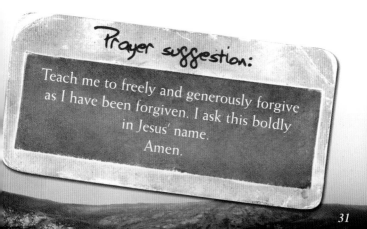

Prayer suggestion:
Teach me to freely and generously forgive as I have been forgiven. I ask this boldly in Jesus' name.
Amen.

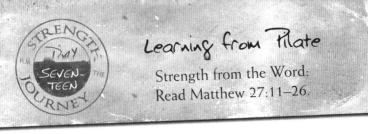

Learning from Pilate

Strength from the Word:
Read Matthew 27:11–26.

I am your servant; give me discernment that I may understand your statutes.

Psalm 119:125

Some choices we face seem too big for us to make. They may affect a great number of people. They may potentially lead us into temptation. They may affect our congregation or our family for decades to come. At times like that we may feel ill-equipped to make a decision. It can be tempting to throw our hands in the air and say, "I'm not touching this one!"

As Jesus stood between Pontius Pilate and an angry crowd, Pilate had to make a decision. The crowd shouted for Christ's death, but Pilate couldn't find any legitimate charges. In the end, Pilate chose this response (Matthew 27:24):

> **When Pilate saw that he was getting nowhere, but that instead an uproar was starting, he took water and washed his hands in front of the crowd. "I am innocent of this man's blood," he said. "It is your responsibility!"**

In one sense there was no decision to make. Jesus *had* to be crucified for the salvation of the world. But neither Pilate nor anyone else there that day knew that with absolute certainty. For Pilate, this was a gut-wrenching decision. He opted to throw his hands in the air and say, "I'm not touching this one!" By submitting to Pilate's verdict, Jesus responded, "I'm handling this one!"

So how do we have the strength to deal with the gut-wrenching decisions in our lives? Scripture gives us clues:

- Seek God's wisdom in dealing with the situation (Proverbs 3:13–18).
- If time permits, consult God-wise people you know (Proverbs 15:22).
- Pray, but then listen for God's direction (Isaiah 30:20–21).
- If the outcome causes sin, remember that sin is never God's will (1 Thessalonians 4:3).
- If you feel you're not the right person to deal with it, don't wash your hands of the situation; rather, offer to assist a better decision maker (Proverbs 12:15).
- And rest in the fact that Jesus has washed our sins away in his blood, shed on the cross, and wants to guide us in all our decision making (Hebrews 13:20–21).

Prayer suggestion:

I want to make decisions according to your will, Lord. Intervene and guide me as I make choices, for then I can rest in peace, knowing your hand is guiding me.
Amen.

> *Let's go to Bethlehem and see this thing that has happened.*
>
> *Luke 2:15*

I'm not an expert shepherd, nor do I play one on TV, but I trust the less-than-sheepish reports I hear about the four-legged animals. Basically, sheep are . . . how can I say this nicely? They're about as bright as a burned out 20-watt light bulb. (I should warn you that tomorrow's Bible reading tells us that *we* are like sheep!)

So if sheep are a few peas short of a casserole, how smart are shepherds? Certainly each has his or her own intellectual level, but the second chapter of Luke tells us about some incredibly smart shepherds.

One night an angel appeared before them, up close and personal! Obviously, they were shocked and afraid. The angel calmed them as he told about the promised Messiah, newly born in a nearby town. Then an angel choir sang praise to God in response to his awesome gift.

When the angels left, the shepherds had a choice. They could go back to counting sheep until they fell asleep. Or they could say to one another, "Let's go to Bethlehem and see this thing that has happened, which the Lord has told us about" (Luke 2:15). That was the right and intelligent decision. And it was just what they did.

Do you find yourself waiting to seek the Lord or worship him until the time is convenient or you're with the "right" group of people? Do you rely on your intellect to figure out how to respond to the presence of Jesus Christ in your life? If so, that may not be the best decision!

When the shepherds heard about their Savior's presence, they immediately went to bask in his company. Following their time with Jesus, they took on the roles of *angels* (which means "messengers") as they told others about who and what they had seen and experienced. Strengthened by Christ's presence, they couldn't keep the good news to themselves.

Those shepherds were not only wise in the choice they made, they were faithful in worshiping the Messiah, the Christ, the Savior. And his presence strengthened them for the journey that followed.

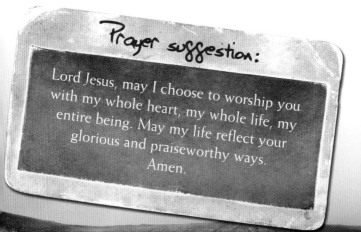

Prayer suggestion:

Lord Jesus, may I choose to worship you with my whole heart, my whole life, my entire being. May my life reflect your glorious and praiseworthy ways. Amen.

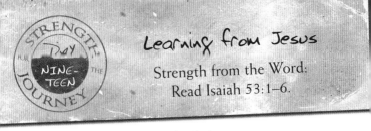
By his wounds we are healed.

Isaiah 53:5

Many Bibles use a title or heading for Isaiah 53 that reads something like *The Suffering and Glory of the Servant.* The words of this chapter foretell the suffering and death of Jesus Christ for the sins and salvation of the world. The message takes us straight to the cross of our Savior, impacting our lives with all the force of a Roman nail being hammered into a splintery cross.

It's in Jesus' journey to Calvary's cross that we miraculously receive strength for our own journey to his cross and to faith in what he did there. In that cross, we receive strength as we learn more about his deep love for us, his commitment to us (Isaiah 53:2–3):

> *He grew up before him like a tender shoot, and like a root out of dry ground. He had no beauty or majesty to attract us to him, nothing in his appearance that we should desire him. He was despised and rejected by men, a man of sorrows, and familiar with suffering.*

We receive strength in learning what he endured for us (Isaiah 53:4–5):

> *Surely he took up our infirmities and carried our sorrows. . . . But he was pierced for our*

transgressions, he was crushed for our iniquities; the punishment that brought us peace was upon him, and by his wounds we are healed.

We receive strength as we stand in wonder and awe, learning how he took upon himself the Father's wrath for every one of our scandalous sins (Isaiah 53:4):

Yet we considered him stricken by God, smitten by him, and afflicted.

We receive strength in realizing we brought nothing to the salvation table but our sins. The forgiveness, strength, and salvation that are ours have come to us, undeserved gifts of our Savior, who took our sin upon himself (Isaiah 53:5–6):

By his wounds we are healed. We all, like sheep, have gone astray, each of us has turned to his own way; and the Lord has laid on him the iniquity of us all.

Fall on your knees at the foot of his cross. Take it all in. Pray. Repent. Receive forgiveness. Give thanks. Worship. Be strengthened in your journey by his sacrifice of grace.

Prayer suggestion:

Let the Holy Spirit lead you as you pray today.

Strength from God's Word as I Make Choices

Over the next two days, begin to commit the following Scripture to memory. Allow the Holy Spirit to transform these faith-strengthening words from head knowledge to heart knowledge. Sink your mind and faith into these words from the books of Psalms and Proverbs:

> *Look to the LORD and his strength;*
> *seek his face always.*
> *Psalm 105:4*

> *Trust in the LORD with all your heart*
> *and lean not on your own understanding;*
> *in all your ways acknowledge him,*
> *and he will make your paths straight.*
> *Proverbs 3:5–6*

Praise be to the God and Father of our Lord Jesus Christ, the Father of compassion and the God of all comfort, who comforts us in all our troubles, so that we can comfort those in any trouble with the comfort we ourselves have received from God. For just as the sufferings of Christ flow over into our lives, so also through Christ our comfort overflows.

2 Corinthians 1:3–5

Strength for Experiencing Change

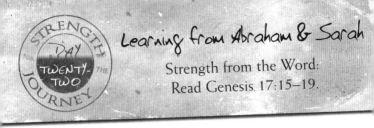

Learning from Abraham & Sarah

Strength from the Word:
Read Genesis 17:15–19.

STRENGTH FOR THE JOURNEY

DAY TWENTY-TWO

Trust in the LORD with all your heart and lean not on your own understanding.

Proverbs 3:5

God transformed Abraham and Sarah—at first laughers and doubters—into trusting, useful servants in fulfilling his salvation plan.

Remember God's revelation to Abraham that he at age 100 and his 90-year-old wife, Sarah, would have a baby? Remember the way Sarah laughed at this news? And she wasn't alone. Abraham also laughed at the Lord's words, even as he lay prostrate at God's feet in worship.

God went on to promise that Abraham would father many nations. More promises followed! God also said, "I will establish my covenant as an everlasting covenant between me and you and your descendants after you for the generations to come, to be your God and the God of your descendants after you" (Genesis 17:7).

In time, God turned Abraham and Sarah's hearts from doubt to trust. God strengthened his people's faith, removing their doubts, and putting the pure laughter of worship and faith into their mouths. (In fact, their son's name, Isaac, means "laughter.") Despite their sin and unbelief, God used Abraham and Sarah in his plan to send the world's Savior.

But what about our own doubt-drenched responses to God's promises and instructions? Do you feel weak at times when it comes to trusting God—taking him at his word?

The Bible is filled with words of instruction, correction, and promise. Unfortunately, our sinful minds too often rely on our own poor reasoning ability rather than on God's perfect words of life.

God loves transforming hearts and minds from fear to faith; he loves bringing us to fall facedown before his Word with reverent awe and respect. God offers to change our hearts from doubt to trust.

If you're struggling with doubts that make you question God's Word or will, seek out his answers as you pray and as you search Scripture deeply and daily. Seek out the counsel of the faithful people God has placed in your life. Your Savior wants to share his perfect will with you as he builds your trust in him.

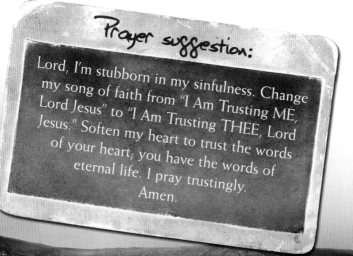

Prayer suggestion:

Lord, I'm stubborn in my sinfulness. Change my song of faith from "I Am Trusting ME, Lord Jesus" to "I Am Trusting THEE, Lord Jesus." Soften my heart to trust the words of your heart; you have the words of eternal life. I pray trustingly. Amen.

Learning from Joseph

Strength from the Word:
Read Matthew 1:18–25.

> *I the LORD do not change.*
>
> *Malachi 3:6*

Joseph, the carpenter from small-town Nazareth, dealt with some big-time changes in a short period of time. Consider the changes he faced:

- His mind changed from trusting Mary to doubting her faithfulness to him.
- He explored ways of changing his commitment to their relationship.
- An angel informed him that the change in Mary was from the Holy Spirit and not from another human father.
- He learned God had chosen him to be the stepfather to the promised Messiah. (Quite a change in status!)
- His life changed drastically when Mary gave birth and he entered fatherhood.

Throughout our lives, we all pass through times of change. Like Joseph, we need God-ordained strength during those times as we journey through life, because . . .

Change is usually	Costly.
Change is mostly	Hard and intimidating.
Change calls for	Action, not passivity.
Change is often	Necessary.
Change should be	God-directed and good.
Change can be	Exciting.

Joseph no doubt understood that acrostic description of change. How about you? Is your small corner of the world about to undergo a big change? In times of change we can lean on the God who empowered Joseph to face such huge changes. We can learn from his example of faithfulness in allowing God to direct his path.

Joseph likely reminded himself of God's past faithfulness in his own life and the lives of those who had gone before him. While he undoubtedly faced ridicule and rejection from many friends, neighbors, and perhaps even family members, the Lord led him through each of the changes and challenges he faced and on into a joyful calling beyond anything he ever could have anticipated earlier in his lifetime.

If you are staring an unwelcome change square in the face today, rejoice that God does not change—and neither does his faithfulness (Malachi 3:6)! Lean on him. Rely on him. Trust in him. No one who puts their hope in our changeless Savior-God is ever disappointed.

Prayer suggestion:

Changeless God, grant me wisdom and peace as changes bombard my life. Lead the way, directing me through all the changes of life and into the changeless eternity of my heavenly home.
Amen.

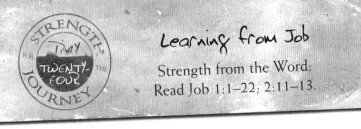

Learning from Job

STRENGTH
FOR THE
JOURNEY

DAY
TWENTY-
FOUR

Strength from the Word:
Read Job 1:1–22; 2:11–13.

> *I know that my Redeemer lives.*
> *Job 19:25*

Job and his wife suffered their own season of grief. They enjoyed ten children, great wealth, and a blessed life. But all that disappeared in a single day, possibly the most horrific day one couple has endured in all of history. All ten children were killed. They lost their crops and cattle and, with that, their income. Their world crumbled.

The Bible describes Job as a blameless (not sinless) and upright man who loved the Lord and hated evil. After all this happened, Job's faith stood firm, even as Job himself grieved. He praised God's name while he wallowed in the deepest depths of grief. "The LORD gave and the LORD has taken away; may the name of the LORD be praised" (Job 1:21).

Job's heart wasn't callous; it ached with the loss of his family and all he had. Like we ourselves in time of trouble, Job wanted answers to his "Why?" questions. But in the midst of it all, he trusted in the presence and promises of the Lord, who had so richly blessed him. He held on to the sure and certain hope of the resurrection of the dead—centuries before Jesus, the Redeemer, was born. Job prophesied: "I know that my Redeemer lives, and that in the end he will stand upon the earth. And after my skin has been destroyed, yet in my flesh I will see God" (Job 19:25–26).

We all have or will someday journey through a season of grief. And although we may find ourselves weak emotionally and physically as we walk the path of loss and grief, we need not grieve as "those . . . who have no hope" (1 Thessalonians 4:13). God's strength can carry us forward and help us persevere, just as it sustained Job.

If you're suffering in a season of grief right now, you may find it difficult to wrap your hands around that truth. If so, won't you allow God's hands to hold you close as he confirms to you his gifts of life, hope, and love through your living and resurrected Savior, Jesus Christ?

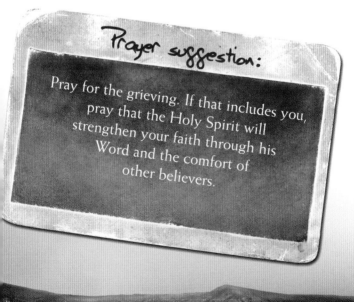

Prayer suggestion:

Pray for the grieving. If that includes you, pray that the Holy Spirit will strengthen your faith through his Word and the comfort of other believers.

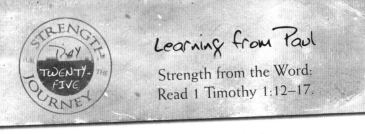
> *I thank Christ Jesus our Lord, who has given
> me strength.*
>
> *1 Timothy 1:12*

What to do with sinners. That issue has plagued the church ever since the Pharisees mocked Jesus for spending time with the *sinners and prostitutes*. Sadly, Jesus' followers today all too often forget that we're part of that group of sinners whom Jesus loves—and that his amazing grace has changed who we once were to who we are now. *Only* that grace could have done it, and *only* that grace can continue to do it.

The apostle Paul once called himself "the worst of sinners" (1 Timothy 1:16). Yet Jesus brought Paul from disgrace. Before his Savior changed his heart and life, Paul murdered Christ's followers. And yet God chose Paul to build Christ's kingdom.

God strengthened Paul for this mission in three ways, making it possible for Paul to endure. First, he surrounded Paul with men of faith to lead and mentor him (Acts 9:11–19). Second, he gave Paul three years of solitude as he broke away from his former way of life. Paul spent this time in the Hebrew Scriptures and in prayer, as God prepared him for the challenges and joys of his new calling (Galatians 1:11–24). And third, the Holy Spirit encouraged Paul to dedicate his life to knowing Christ and the power of Christ's resurrection (Philippians 3:7–14).

The change in Paul's life was miraculous and astounding, yet no less than the change brought about in our own lives when the Holy Spirit created faith within us. Accepted into God's family by grace, we now also can accept others in love, growing in unity with them as together we form the family of Christ.

Paul, the forgiven and adopted child of God, once wrote (1 Timothy 1:12–14):

> *I thank Christ Jesus our Lord, who has given me strength, that he considered me faithful, appointing me to his service. Even though I was once a blasphemer and a persecutor and a violent man, I was shown mercy. . . . The grace of our Lord was poured out on me abundantly, along with the faith and love that are in Christ Jesus.*

Prayer suggestion:

Lord, you are the God who abundantly pours out his grace on me, strengthening me for ministry in your name. Thank you! Amen.

Learning from Jesus

Strength from the Word:
Read Matthew 6:25–34.

Therefore I tell you, do not worry about your life.
Matthew 6:25

If you are looking for the strength to accept change, there's no better place to look than to the very words of Jesus, who endured so many enormous changes throughout the journey he took from heaven to earth and back to heaven again. He's the one who brings good and godly changes to our lives still today, making us new creations in himself (2 Corinthians 5:17).

Consider, for example, Jesus' words from his Sermon on the Mount as you think about making and dealing with changes in your life. Be blessed as Jesus speaks to you and your situation:

> *Give your entire attention to what God is doing right now, and don't get worked up about what may or may not happen tomorrow. God will help you deal with whatever hard things come up when the time comes.*
> *Matthew 6:34 THE MESSAGE*

> *You're blessed when you're at the end of your rope. With less of you there is more of God and his rule.*
> *You're blessed when you feel you've lost what is most dear to you. Only then can you be embraced by the One most dear to you.*

You're blessed when you're content with just who you are—no more, no less. That's the moment you find yourselves proud owners of everything that can't be bought.

You're blessed when you've worked up a good appetite for God. He's food and drink in the best meal you'll ever eat.

You're blessed when you care. At the moment of being "care-full," you find yourselves cared for.

You're blessed when you get your inside world— your mind and heart—put right. Then you can see God in the outside world.

You're blessed when you can show people how to cooperate instead of compete or fight. That's when you discover who you really are, and your place in God's family.

You're blessed when your commitment to God provokes persecution. The persecution drives you even deeper into God's kingdom.

Matthew 5:3–10 THE MESSAGE

The place where your treasure is, is the place you will most want to be, and end up being.

Matthew 6:21 THE MESSAGE

Prayer suggestion:

Jesus, teach me through every moment of change as I journey through life following you. Amen.

Strength from God's Word as I Experience Change

Over the next two days, begin to commit the following Scripture to memory. Allow the Holy Spirit to transform these faith-strengthening words from head knowledge to heart knowledge. Sink your mind and faith into these words from the psalmist David and the prophet Malachi:

> *The LORD is my light and my salvation—*
> *whom shall I fear?*
> *The LORD is the stronghold of my life—*
> *of whom shall I be afraid?*
>
> *Psalm 27:1*

> **I the LORD do not change.**
>
> *Malachi 3:6*

We pray that you'll have the strength to stick it out over the long haul—not the grim strength of gritting your teeth but the glory-strength God gives. It is strength that endures the unendurable and spills over into joy, thanking the Father who makes us strong enough to take part in everything bright and beautiful that he has for us.

Colossians 1:10–12 THE MESSAGE

Strength for Continuing the Journey

Learning from Elijah

Strength from the Word:
Read 1 Kings 19:3–9.

> *Get up and eat, for the journey is too much for you.*
> *1 Kings 19:7*

Have you experienced moments when you stood unwaveringly on the foundation of God's Word, God's strength? Do you find those moments seem to come in waves—sometimes you're faithful and strong, other times weak and faithless? Up and down, up and down.

Elijah's life and faith walk stand out in a crowd as an example of just such a life story. Elijah served as a bold voice for the Lord, unashamedly proclaiming God's will no matter what or whom he faced. He audaciously defended God's honor against the 450 prophets of Baal on Mount Carmel (1 Kings 17–18).

But after scoring a great victory, Elijah hits a wall. Coming off the tremendous God-as-Lord-and-King event on Mount Carmel, Elijah finds himself running for his life from one wicked woman—Queen Jezebel. Discouraged, dejected, and depressed, he escapes into the wilderness where he plops down and prays that he might die. Then, exhausted, he falls asleep (1 Kings 19:1–5).

We might suspect we have come to the end of the story, a distressing and doubt-filled end. But the Lord is not about to leave his dearly loved servant in that state. He sends an angel to awaken Elijah, providing bread and water for him. After eating, Elijah falls asleep again. The angel comes back with more sustenance, saying, "Get up and eat, for the journey is too much for you" (1 Kings 19:7). Scripture tells us "[Elijah] got up and ate and drank. Strengthened by that food, he traveled forty days and forty nights until he reached Horeb, the mountain of God" (1 Kings 19:8). There, God gave his prophet a mountaintop experience—quite literally!

It's no different for us. The journey is too much for us, too—on our own. But we don't travel alone. Our Savior nourishes us; his presence sustains us. He brings us to the mountaintop of his Word and the precious promises in that Word. When we're downhearted, he gives us traveling companions to encourage us in the faith. Relying on God's strength and provision, we're able to continue. Sustained by his love, we will one day finish the journey!

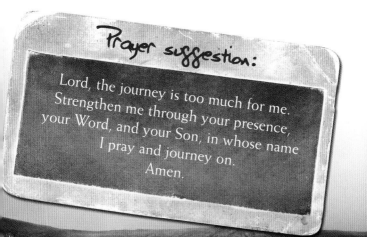

Prayer suggestion:

Lord, the journey is too much for me. Strengthen me through your presence, your Word, and your Son, in whose name I pray and journey on. Amen.

Learning from Isaiah

Strength from the Word:
Read Isaiah 6:1–8.

FOR STRENGTH
DAY
TWIRTY
THE
JOURNEY

> ### Here am I. Send me!
> #### Isaiah 6:8

Isaiah's divine call into the ministry—to serve as a prophet of the Lord—is dramatic and powerful. Isaiah receives an amazing vision of the Lord in all his heavenly glory. Isaiah sees and hears angels proclaiming (Isaiah 6:3):

> ### Holy, holy, holy is the LORD Almighty;
> ### the whole earth is full of his glory.

Isaiah responds as any sinner must in the presence of a holy, perfect God. He realizes his imperfection, his sin, in the presence of the sinless One. Isaiah cries out, "Woe to me! . . . I am ruined! For I am a man of unclean lips, and I live among a people of unclean lips, and my eyes have seen the King, the LORD Almighty" (Isaiah 6:5).

Isaiah confesses his unworthiness and sin in the presence of the Almighty. The Lord responds immediately, sending an angel to touch Isaiah's unclean lips with a live coal taken from heaven's high altar. He says, "See, this has touched your lips; your guilt is taken away and your sin atoned for" (Isaiah 6:7).

The Lord forgives the sins of his servant and in doing so prepares the prophet to answer a profound question. Isaiah writes:

Then I heard the voice of the Lord saying, "Whom shall I send? And who will go for us?"
Isaiah 6:8

And Isaiah responds, "Here am I. Send me!"

Sin and its accompanying guilt sap our strength. They wound our service. They take the breath out of our relationships. But the full and free forgiveness the Lord pours out on us, his repentant servants, restores our strength, heals our service, and repairs our relationships. The miraculous gift of forgiveness readies us and arms us to journey with the Lord and for him.

The Lord asks today, "Whom shall I send? And who will go for us?" Washed clean—forgiven—we can confidently and joyfully respond in the presence of the Almighty, "Here I am. Send me!"

Prayer suggestion:

Heavenly Father, through the life, death, and resurrection of Jesus, your forgiveness has freed me for service in your kingdom. Help me to gladly forgive those who have sinned against me. Forgiven, I stand before you ready for the journey. Here I am, Lord. Send me. Amen.

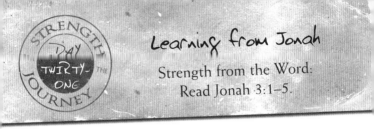

STRENGTH
DAY
THIRTY-
ONE
JOURNEY
THE

Learning from Jonah

Strength from the Word:
Read Jonah 3:1–5.

> *In my distress I called to the LORD, and he answered me.*
>
> *Jonah 2:2*

If you know the story of Jonah, you'll recall that God called him to preach to the ungodly people of Nineveh. Jonah refused, instead boarding a ship headed in the opposite direction. Then came the storm, and Jonah knew it had come because of his disobedience. At Jonah's insistence, his fellow travelers threw him overboard. Then entered the great fish to enjoy some Jonah-flavored junk food.

But Jonah lived to pray about his situation in Chapter 2. As Jonah's prayer ended, you will likely remember, the Book records the ever-so-disgusting-fish-vomiting scene that land-ed Jonah back on dry ground. Jonah then travels to Ninevah to preach. And he finds that the people believe his news about the one true God.

But that is not the end of the story! There's a fourth and final chapter. Did you realize that even though Jonah finally obeyed and God worked through him, Jonah wasn't happy about it? In fact, the prophet pouted! After the Ninevites repented and believed, Jonah prayed, "I knew that you are a gracious and compassionate God, slow to anger and abound-ing in love, a God who relents from sending calamity.

Now, O LORD, take away my life, for it is better for me to die than to live" (Jonah 4:2–3).

Perhaps Jonah figured that the Israelites back home might disown him for sharing God's grace with the hated Ninevites. Or perhaps Jonah himself secretly had hoped to see the Ninevites getting the fire and brimstone they had by their sins deserved.

Either way, the Bible never tells us what happens to Jonah. Does he repent and receive forgiveness? Or does prejudice, hatred, and unforgiveness turn his heart to stone?

Jonah's story reminds us to seek God's help in overcoming our own prejudices so we can joyfully share the Good News of Jesus with *all* people—even those we perceive as different from us or threatening to us.

Jonah had it right. God *is* gracious and compassionate, abounding in love. He works in miraculous ways to change hearts so that they beat in sync with his. He has given us the honor of sharing Christ with a world swallowed up by unbelief and sitting in the belly of hopelessness.

Prayer suggestion:

Lord, grant me true joy in sharing you!
Amen.

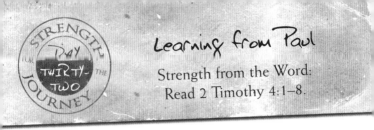

Learning from Paul

Strength from the Word:
Read 2 Timothy 4:1–8.

*I have fought the good fight, I have finished the race,
I have kept the faith.*

2 Timothy 4:7

When we look back on past hardships, it's easy to remember the heartache, as well as the outcome, but to forget the actual journey as the Lord led us *through* the situation. The Lord used the pen of the prophet Isaiah to remind his people, "When you pass *through* the waters, I will be with you; and when you pass *through* the rivers, they will not sweep over you. When you walk *through* the fire, you will not be burned; the flames will not set you ablaze" (Isaiah 43:2, emphasis added).

The Lord not only promises his presence, but he also vows to bring his people *through* the difficulties they're facing. He's present *and* active during the times of our struggle and stress.

That truth holds true even at our life journey's end. Psalm 23:4 reads, "Even though I walk through the valley of the shadow of death I will fear no evil, for you are with me."

The psalmist speaks of walking *through* the shadow of death. God brings Christ's followers through life, through death's shadow, and then, by grace alone, through the gates of heaven.

The apostle Paul experienced this in countless times of difficulty. Toward the end of his life on earth, he wrote poignantly, "I have fought the good fight, I have finished the race, I have kept the faith. Now there is in store for me the crown of righteousness, which the Lord, the righteous Judge, will award to me on that day—and not only to me, but also to all who have longed for his appearing" (2 Timothy 4:7–8).

Paul knew his Savior had brought him *through* a lifetime of adventures. And now Jesus would take him through death itself, and on into a perfect eternity in heaven—God's ultimate gift of grace. There Paul would receive the crown of righteousness, all because Jesus had journeyed *through* life, *through* death, and *through* a tomb. Christ's gift of eternal life in the perfection of heaven came not only to Paul, but it comes to *all* who place their Spirit-created faith in Jesus Christ as their Savior.

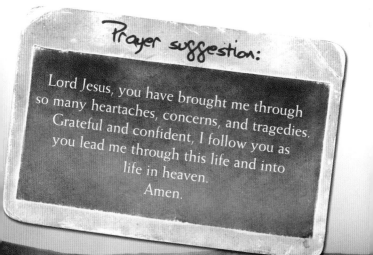

Prayer suggestion:

Lord Jesus, you have brought me through so many heartaches, concerns, and tragedies. Grateful and confident, I follow you as you lead me through this life and into life in heaven.
Amen.

STRENGTH
DAY
TWIRTY-
THREE
FOR
JOURNEY

Learning from Jesus

Strength from the Word:
Read Luke 9:51.

When the days drew near for him [Jesus] to be taken up, he set his face to go to Jerusalem.
Luke 9:51 ESV

It's a great visual. Jesus knew what lay ahead: betrayal, ridicule, torture, hatred, and ultimately death on a cross. However, focused on the goal before him, strengthened by his Father's love, and empowered by his love for us and our need for a Savior, he "set his face to go to Jerusalem." With great resolve he continued his journey.

Jesus was able to do this because he saw beyond the cross. He knew he would see the sun rise on Resurrection morning, announcing to those in mourning that the Son had risen, never to set again. And Jesus foresaw a reunion with his Father in heaven forty days after his resurrection. His journey would most certainly not end in death. Rather, it would introduce new life into the lives of everyone who placed their trust in him. And so he set his face to go to Jerusalem and to the cross that awaited him there.

Stop. Who or what is in your face right now? Name names. Consider appointments on your calendar. Think about the decisions and the difficulties you face. And then . . . set your face on Jerusalem.

Realize that the people, appointments, and decisions you will face in the coming hours or days won't disappear. The harsh realities of life won't suddenly turn into fairy tales. Yet things will change because you'll be changed by the change-less God.

The One who changed history by hanging around with sinners and later hanging on a cross to forgive sins—that One will change how your journey pans out. You'll be strengthened by Jesus Christ, who himself was weakened by torture and was lifeless when carried to the tomb. You'll receive strength for your journey because on that death trap of a cross he crushed Satan's power, ransacked hell, and shattered the grip of death. And now he hands you the key to heaven.

Heaven's glorious strength is yours. So set your face on Jerusalem's Jesus, and he'll provide strength for your journey.

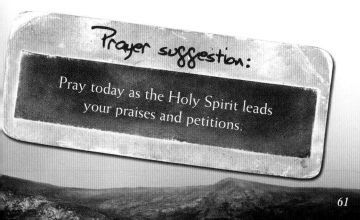

Prayer suggestion:

Pray today as the Holy Spirit leads your praises and petitions.

Strength from God's Word as I Continue the Journey with My Savior

Over the next two days, begin to commit the following Scripture to memory. Allow the Holy Spirit to transform these faith-strengthening words from head knowledge to heart knowledge. Sink your mind and faith into these words from Psalms and the writings of the apostle Paul:

> *For the LORD is good*
> *and his love endures forever;*
> *his faithfulness continues*
> *through all generations.*
> *Psalm 100:5*

> *So then, just as you received Christ Jesus*
> *as Lord, continue to live in him,*
> *rooted and built up in him,*
> *strengthened in the faith as you were taught,*
> *and overflowing with thankfulness.*
> *Colossians 2:6–7*

STRENGTH FOR THE JOURNEY

Blessed are those whose strength is in you,
who have set their hearts on pilgrimage.
Psalm 84:5

We pray that you'll have the strength
to stick it out over the long haul—
not the grim strength of gritting your teeth
but the glory-strength God gives.
It is strength that endures the unendurable and spills over
into joy, thanking the Father who makes us strong enough
to take part in everything bright and beautiful
that he has for us.
Colossians 1:10–12 THE MESSAGE

The LORD is the strength of his people,
a fortress of salvation for his anointed one.
Psalm 28:8

He will keep you strong to the end,
so that you will be blameless
on the day of our Lord Jesus Christ.
God, who has called you into fellowship
with his Son Jesus Christ our Lord, is faithful.
1 Corinthians 1:8–9

Now to him who is able to do immeasurably
more than all we ask or imagine,
according to his power
that is at work within us,
to him be glory in the church
and in Christ Jesus throughout all generations,
for ever and ever! Amen.
Ephesians 3:20–21